Squirrel Monkeys

Written by Jo Windsor

In this book
you will see
squirrel monkeys.

You will see...

tails

jumping

babies

Squirrel monkeys are small monkeys. They have white faces and black noses.

Squirrel monkeys have lots of fur on their ears.

Squirrel monkeys live in
the rainforest.
They live in the tops of the trees.

They like to stay in groups
so they will be safe.
Lots of eyes can look for danger!

*What would
the danger be?*

Squirrel monkeys call to
other monkeys in the group.
This keeps the group together.

But when there is danger,
they will make a big, big noise.
They will bark and scream.

Look out! Look out!

All the monkeys
know there is danger!

Squirrel monkeys like to eat leaves, fruits, seeds, eggs and insects.

When one monkey finds food, the others will come to get it, too.

Food, food! Lots of food over here!

Squirrel monkeys have hands with fingers and thumbs.

They hold on to the branches of the trees.

They have legs that are good for jumping from tree to tree.

They can go very fast.

A squirrel monkey has a long tail.
The tail helps the monkey
hold on to trees.

When it walks along a branch,
it holds on to the branch with its tail.
It will not fall off.

A squirrel monkey
uses its tail to...

hold on to
the tree   Yes? No?

get food   Yes? No?

fly   Yes? No?

A squirrel monkey has
one baby at a time.

When a baby is born,
it holds on to its mother's fur.

It drinks its mother's milk
and sleeps in her fur.

The baby will ride around on the mother's back.

The baby holds on tight!

When the mother is jumping from tree to tree,
the baby will not fall off.

The baby holds on
with its...

tail   Yes? No?

hands and feet Yes? No?

teeth   Yes? No?

The monkeys in the group will help look after the baby until it is six months old.

Index

babies . . 3, 16, 18, 20

danger 8

food 10

jumping 3, 13, 18

living

   in groups . . . 6, 8, 20

tails 3, 14

A yes/no chart

Squirrel monkeys can bark. Yes? No?

A squirrel monkey has a red nose. Yes? No?

Squirrel monkeys live in the water. Yes? No?

Squirrel monkeys eat insects and fruit. Yes? No?

Squirrel monkeys eat people. Yes? No?

Squirrel monkeys are good at jumping. Yes? No?

Word Bank

branch

ears

eggs

face

fingers

fruit

insects

seeds

thumb